Other books of poetry
by David Shapiro

JANUARY

POEMS FROM DEAL

A MAN HOLDING AN ACOUSTIC PANEL

THE PAGE-TURNER

LATENESS

TO AN IDEA

A BOOK OF POEMS

TO AN IDEA
A BOOK OF POEMS

DAVID SHAPIRO

THE OVERLOOK PRESS
Woodstock, New York

ACKNOWLEDGEMENTS

Some of these poems have appeared in *The Paris Review, The Colum-bia Review, Z, Padan Aran, Broadway: An Anthology of Poets and Painters, CAPS Anthology, New Directions Annual, New York Arts Journal, The Iowa Review, The Poetry Mailing List, The William and Mary Review, TriQuarterly, New Observations,* and *Sulfur.* "A Song" appeared as a Poetry Mailing List pamphlet with photographs by Rudy Burckhardt. "To An Idea" appeared in *House X* (Rizzoli International Publications Inc.). "Unwritten" appeared as a Lapp Princess Press pamphlet with drawings by Lucio Pozzi. Some lines in "Those Who Must Stay Indoors" are after the *Field Book of Natural History.*

First published by Tusk/Overlook in 1986 by
The Overlook Press
Lewis Hollow Road

Copyright © 1983 by David Shapiro

Library of Congress Cataloging in Publication Data

Shapiro, David, 1947-
    To an idea.

    I. Title
PS3569.H34T6 1983   811:.54   82-2238
ISBN 0-87951-176-1 (cloth)
ISBN 0-87951-181-8 (deluxe)
ISBN 0-87951-255-5 (paper)

Manufactured in the United States of America

CONTENTS

TO AN IDEA

A BOOK OF POEMS

FALLING UPWARDS

A certain violinist had a beautiful violin
But before he had had time to play her long and listen
To her tones as such, he was compelled to renounce music
And sell her, and go on a far journey, and leave his violin
    in the hands of the violin case.

What was there to do? It is said You cannot live life in
    quarter tones.
What was there to do? It is said you cannot live your life
    in silence.
What was there to do? It is said you cannot live your life
    playing scales.
What was there to do? It is said you cannot live your life listening
    to the Americans.

What was there to do. It is said you cannot live your
    life in your room and not go out.
What was there to do? It is said music disobeys
And reaches the prince's courtyard ever farther than smell
    and grits its notes like teeth and gives us food and drink.
And orders a fire to be lighted, famished silk to hang over it
    and repetitions to be sharpened.

What was there to do? It is said it is the violinists who
    do not sleep.
What was there to do? It is said we think and don't think;
    we are asleep.
What was there to do? It is said music sinks into the mire up
    to its neck, wants to crawl out, but cannot.
What was there to do? It is said the violin was a swan,
    seized the boy, falling upwards to some height above the earth.

UNWRITTEN

1

On the border of the illusion
Phaedo condemned the death of Socrates
But in so doing he missed a single day
And rendered his own judgment like an entertained
   breeze
It was a jailer who introduced us
He was a jailer with no appetite
And you know how fire is delivered
By children frittering it away in frozen speech
Men call this pleasure like a place of rapport
But it — is it bliss to juggle the body
Like a house with great pain persuaded to stand
The swans change a lot before they discover
   gods they serve
He sat on his bed and had time to say a big thing
The wind ascending at the corners of the
   cardboard world

2

On the border of the illusion
Socrates and Phaedrus made a shimmering detour
They pleased themselves in their descent
On the border of the illusion where they
   reassembled the cut sentences
Phaedrus applauded the truth of leaving
But today my shoes are all worn out
Socrates said I want you very much
But try to find another time to sit together
Phaedrus was the pleased student shadow and fresh
   air
Socrates was going to the young rhythm
I want to repay this very good but tell me
Do you believe in this fabulous affair
It is he, it is me, it is charm in lieu of sleep
I am surrounded by the summer you sent me,
   your throat on this stained floor

On the border of the illusion (at the very edge)
Socrates said Let's go Crito obsess yourselves
You were a slave with tender hands and dwindled too
Sometimes we'll come back and give out poison
Now it's all boiled up and just as ready
One likes to drink and walk and having drunk
You feel those heavy weights like a dog
The lips of Socrates were very peaceful then
You had your lips next to me drinking and having drunk
You covered up your closest friends with a mind
It was cut like sails with the same razor
It was ice and radiant touching to be him
Now we owe a rooster to forget it would be impossible
In a convulsive movement time says time and closes your
    eyes

TO AN IDEA

I wanted to start *Ex Nihilo*
I mean as a review of sorts.
It's too much of a burst for some,
Too unanalyzably simple for others,
As one called perspective that vicious
Doctrine, but is it: to know nothing,
To taste something, dazzled by absence,
By your chair, by the chair of Salome?
Or yet another familiar dedication:
To an idea, writ in water,
To wild flesh, on the surface alone.
To you who carried me like mail
From one house to another.
Now the cars go past the lake, as if copying could exist.
The signs shine, through the Venetian blinds.

TO INDUSTRY

I took a sewer tour of America
With Jean Valjean a comic older poet
His poem was tunnels
And mine the inability to follow.

Vade retro mimesis. He cried
And mimesis followed (a mime).
Vade retro, mimesis!
Vade retro, mimesis, to profile, frontality, and back.

What I could do was rise up out of the tunnel
like a bird and as a bird
delightfully above that poet-bird's head
enjoy my feathers despite the fears of height

And definitely exceed in verticality
what I had lost in horizontal fight
And like a scarlet tanager I fell
and was kicked out on the earth as a man
　　as an idea

AN EXERCISE IN FUTILITY

I met an university professor in an antique land
Who said: In my hand is a cartographer's dream,
The country which blurred genres.
                    To release its secret of release

Under the cartons of cardboard script, the discoverers, the learners
And one's own fingers exploring the dumb thick maps.
Oh secret love, heterodoxy, self-deceit,
You have reckoned without the host and taken the shadow for
    credulity
And dreamt all the rapports, at the foot of the airmail letter.
The nicety of a hair, the pleasures of exit
Writhing in passages,
Alive to the needle, down clever arches, hunting you like a bluejay.

You whom I had loved for years like a monumental door leading to
An exterior interior: to get to this door you climbed a tiny, tinny
    podium
And there two mirrors poured into each other
In a maroon room covered up with dust of bricks and books:
But for you the mirrors rushing into each other had lost something.

I saw he had no temperament to speak of —
A fan instead of a typewriter; a tree that was watery air
Buoying the bright horizon; three other countries rolled up beside
    him;
And on the other side of him, a picture of him
Where he begs, student-wise, another sage,
For another scheme, like a part of the bending tree
Of desire. The beaks surround him
Surround us and lunge out of us like a wish.

Snowflakes bewildered the upper edge of things.
The bridge is not an argument,
Nor is it a bridge, in a sense.
The birds are flying buttresses.
No impedimenta on the bridge;
No traveller on the boardwalk; two hands are folded above the tree.

SPHINX SKIN

In that remotest sky
where the only note is sky
or not at all

needing the mildest comfort
of the hand or not all
or not all again, see

if Zeno is correct we'll never get there

or halfway there

This was to be the hologram of our
love not so whole

in that sky, where all details
begin, begin to be ravaged

mixing with and changing to snow

Here then is nothing but
thought and closures

Two houses embrace
Night disastrous lionized features
    its relapses

So this was the music they rejected
an analysis so poignant it could have
included them
Intemperate or hesitant smiles
and sunny throat
It is understandable if perception
doesn't want us around
It could happen and it did
impenetrable as any door

eyes closed always on the world
The day was your commandment
a work in Latin resisting to have to be everyone
the you Oh to advise things
Ancient activity head and money
as a piano in a clump of chord clusters
ink sun so cloudy a bit Chinese
ink that wanders through Eternity

Forget it just become conscious
think about thinking Just think about it
What you're doing is an umbrella
I'm going to push your face in That's a cliché
Not a ceiling, not a floor
as a sun dwells on a dictation machine

Ballet stars are sleeping in their shoes
   Hair of your head pressed against hair of my head
Fluttering eyelids of incoming ink
Taking down sentences to freeze the night
Which otherwise might have unlocked itself in secrets
Calculatingly disarmed from the starting point

If I continued to sleep in the right way
        This would become dangerous to the sleeper
The door is not a window:
Don't get between the sleeper and his sleep
Giving birth to reflexes for the writing reader

It was and it was not
My dimensionlessness is
A sycamore that begins in bark and ends in the nude
Ageless bracelets taught me the laws of foreshortening
There is only one *Fieldbook of Natural History*
Only one fairy tale only one Gaius Valerius
Only one facsimile
        There are only two characters:
        the writer and the reader

The shadow of the no is on the no
Maybe the afterimage of the shadow of a no
Do you think if the Erectheum cannot last
then this no will last? No

A FRAGMENT OF RELIEF

It doesn't matter but it does
Some picture by a painter on wood
A snake and another dog
Apollo rises
He embraces a huge snake
Nothing like this exists
It is doubtful who belongs to the family of the god
Does the god belong
Does the letter belong

Relief of doctors in the form of a shrine
We worry below the representation
Your name
Almost all other names battered
Late work, unique

You ran forward impetuously
As planes pursue planes

I could not carve it out of the American desert
        Therefore
I cut it out of white business paper

THE COUNTER-EXAMPLE

As in Frege's luminous counter-example

Everyone is dead and we will come later in fugue
Or lullaby, according to the mistranslations

Putting ice on the dying woman's lips
Macadam bond is another title

You did not want to paint twisting life in red points
But randomly following the paper, you twisted the lines

Distorted as a man following a dolphin
struggling not to surface but diving to drown

in a drifting wet imperturbability

    The morning star is not the evening star

To the mortal beloved
and to the one of real music

eyes closed always on the world
Poor air, I pull you over me to warm this cold light

But what is closure when we are so open
And what is lack of closure when we are so close

COMMENTARY TEXT COMMENTARY TEXT COMMENTARY TEXT

In the morning, the water fed the sky,
Eyes of another material had been inserted and the hair,
                    gathered into high strands, more carefully
  arranged.
Two more bodies were discovered in the Spanish
forest fire.
Sky like sand, sand like a body
Sun like a breast one faintly outlined
In blue magic marker and bleeding into the margin
Of its own sunny space.

And a stable bridge linking us no longer
August like autumn and the new encyclopedia
Nom de guerre: Nothing.

Nonobservance, nonappearance, noncompletion.

Like the bright male cardinal on the red maple

No man's land and no mistake. No wonder.
Noah's ark nocturne.
Inferno black Purgatorio matte grey Paradise is almost white
Present I flee you
Absent I have you
Your name like landscape written across the middle of the page

HOUSE

In extreme pain
Q meets T
They walk into a house
And later a double exposure is sent to S

Somewhere behind the curtains
Uncertainty is laughing
As you ask the yes or no questions
I am moving towards you by analogy

AN EARLY EGYPTIAN SHIP

1

In ancient Egypt, when a king died
Details were placed inside a boat
To travel the sunny wake of the Underworld
These grew slender and parted the eye
Slit where the lines show and paint the men
Glued like an exact likeness you do not know
Punched like a pinhole in a bending breeze
As sailors say slitting the discerning tree
Between the fingers and then looking
Go, into a hole of space already occupied
Like the skeleton at the party with a
"Skeleton story" and filled in with the
Blank round of adjectives — It is enough
To show how the skeleton ship might be spun along

2

In the twelfth dynasty, when kings began to row
They noticed you hanging over the enormous bow
The squirrel speeded along the grounds
As if in proportion to the simple craft
Guests died placed in their nightly tomb like East and West
Now the sail was hung and a single star replaced
      the sky
It is interesting not to know
And in persistence unimproved like time
The blinds grow larger and the junk
Decorated as if to prevent us from parting
I am tied around you to make you small
Are the blanks filled now? The loud product
Is finished and the quiet result each one might bring
My head has been removed, with your own hands

3

All is illustration when an Egyptian ship
Passes by with the kings of Egypt
You noticed her high bow and the inveterate boat
And the distinguished guests oh now too small
The king is dead but not the tiny models
They were complete in every detail
And suppose we had a soul and travelled
That decisive stream and followed in foamy wake
With seashells in our ears beyond the jetty
The scissor has cut the sail and the Nile
We are dropping in the mist who love the snakes
And features of the hull and how to make them
History is complete but not the sailing ship
We are lost, like pen knives and scissors in a breeze

THE INDEX OF FIRST LINES

Between thirty and forty
Violinists boast of their violins
Like a magnolia in an old home
In the house one asks, Whose house is this, is it mine

The single cup of a house
The Hudson River is a glorious land
The year is closing with nothing behind the veil
Invisible mites level all plants
Click, click, and always in Chinese, click, click
The Palisades with their extrusion and intrusion
The year was closing with nothing behind the veil

Dear friends, there is no cause and effect
I had a will to serve you
As you swerved in your big car

My father and mother lined the returning streets
Ever since the hour they left me for the walk around the Park

Cygnus the Swan is very close but stuck
Like a bluejay that has lost its oak
The typewriter always in front of my bed
For ten years, it never left the bookshelves
But those high words never reached the shelf

Not too gently now I put in another piece of paper
White as a feather or a rabbit or a cypress
Green as heat, and green as the earth her door
Opening on the white water of woman's form
How quickly it dries
One house on the chessboard

In Holland there is not enough room for a mirror
In the wind — many trees — the boy Mozart was frightened
On the lake he could control his remote bed
The year was closing with nothing behind the veil
Dear friends, there is not much cause and effect

In the new street, the art of floating up
The International Tin Symposium, immeasurable pain
It is no insult to say it is like the index of first lines
In the night when I have not lost my hearing
I hear you, your thoughts that went to fight
Your thoughts in my hand like a zone of flowering paper

In the house one asks, Whose house is this, is it mine
This paper is so empty I keep waking up
Inside I play in my light word

The earth will be more precious to you
Now, as it slips under your feet
One of the words that cannot be used again: crystal towns
In the distant water like architecture in the mountains that might
     reflect
The stain growing in the valley's glass
The snow risen beside the unpainted screen of idle windows

A SONG

When a man loves a woman
the words withdraw to the palace
he demands his words and rejoices seeing them neighing
                into his face
the words in whiteness the words race the hasty words
        stand around and excite their breasts

When a man loves a woman
He wraps his coat of words about his shoulders
Scaled with gold and white mountain words
At the same time he fits for wearing both his word and his world

When a man loves a woman
he seizes the strong word with violence and says trembling
Now Oh word never disappearing
Now the world is present and the maximum Actor wrote you (not
   spoken)

When a man loves a woman
the words preside over the pool and the sounding streams
the king of the sky spits and the nymph grace note
of rivers grace note to my mind you know I have preferred
        you alone to all placed you willingly in a part of
        my words

WHEN A MAN LOVES A WOMAN BY PERCY SLEDGE

When a man loves a woman
Hospitals are supplied with beds and clothing
If she is life nearer the front
He is fitted with beds kitchens and dispensaries

When a man
the sick and wounded upon their hands like wagons
He gives his ambulance
he is incapable of keeping up with the troops

When a man
the Indian ambulances are carts drawn by bullocks and mules
Very strongly made they are holding two men
lying down and four sitting up alert as a driver

When a man loves a woman
the wounded man is transferred to a hospital ship
in the comfortable swinging cot in the airy ward
and the ice flies into the hot wind and the bed rises on the shore

Yes when a man loves a woman
the bonds of union are drawn considerably closer
In the War however
the present and the past overlap and the skeleton foot of time

WHEN A MAN LOVES A WOMAN BY PERCY SLEDGE

When a man loves a woman by Percy Sledge
he is like a polygonal block of limestone
She is the city and city wall measuring 2½ meters
Two of his gates are still to some extent preserved

When a man loves a woman
Remains can be traced and the traces are finely ruined
Huge blocked halls arise
Two approaches to the citadel added and blocked on the north

When a man loves a woman a genus of the trees
Parts of the world are fruit
Used for good and light
And the man is called the candlenut

When a man loves a woman
she is the vanishing and the lace and the lake
and the seeds contained in the decorated Museo of "of"
The absent town has a picturesque aspect yes

Yes when a man loves a woman
he wants the ruler who would be noble the Swabian line
His nobles whom he tried to cow by sporadic acts of violence
rebelled against him leaving a will and Sancho and Seville and civil
    war

When a man loves a woman

When a man loves a woman
He has fallen by the art of his stepmother
and drawn apart by frightened automobiles
has satisfied his father's hit-and-run punishment

When a man
he has burdened himself with equal arms
to outstrip the wind on an automobile
like a spy approached the camps of the Greeks daring to
          demand the automobile of Achilles

When a man loves a woman
he beholds her far off like a headquarters
first having pursued her through the void
through the long void with a short arrow

When a man loves a woman
he stops his Toyota and leaps from his front seat
and comes up to her half dead with a safety belt
and his neck being pressed with her foot he wrenches
                    the wrench from her right hand

And dips it shining in his alto jugulo (throat)
When a man loves a woman
moreover he adds these words
You lie stretched out like Italy and the wind shakes her
                    hair flying into the opposing comb

When a man loves a woman
each one withdraws into its own space a signal being given
they plant their spears into the ground
and lean upon their shadows then the mothers pour out with zeal

When a man loves a woman
the unarmed populace and the powerless sold men besiege them
the snowy words lie on the oaken typewriter
the black words follow the combs combing out your hair

When a man loves a woman
then the tiger is hungry
and you who composed the songs of shepherds and were audacious
stop singing beneath the terminal the bus station and the goons
                    (cherish me, Naples!)
and the ninth morning displays you homeless as a funeral offering

When a man loves a woman
his neck is untouched and suddenly the words are humming
            in his carcass like bees
and his dissolved entrails and breaking through the page
and immense clouds of words are drawn out

WHEN A MAN LOVES A WOMAN

When a man loves a woman
he attacks the fleet, which lay concealed
and commands his rejoicing associates to bring fire
and glowing he fills his hand with a burning pain

When a man loves a woman
he knows the sound and trembling flees back
he flies and drives the dark band across the television set
as when a constellation passes over alas cardiologists

When a man loves a woman
they rejoice sprinkled with the blood of his brothers
and exchange their homes and sweet dwelling
and seeking another bed lying beneath another bed

When a man loves a woman
I beg this last favor (pity the seething surface) does she hear
            any words
which when she shall have granted to me
I will dismiss her gratified in my words sisters

When a man loves a woman by Percy Sledge

When a man loves a woman
his right hand is torn from his horse and bears him off
and a story is raised then the window shade presses in on him
and the Venetian blinds beat the air with their slats

When a man loves a woman
grapes increase hair and spontaneous flourishes elsewhere
but the stones are established in the empty globe
whence woman a hardy race was produced

When a man loves a woman
the prospect may feed the hungry mind but the land will not give
also you will ask what depth the trenches
Do not commit the vine even to the light furrow the earth is low

When a man loves a woman
it sinks its roots into the Hall
and for many years strong arms and branches move this way and that
Nor let your yard incline not plant the lazy hazel among the vines
                    nor break the twigs (love the earth)

VENETIAN BLINDS

I have been leading the new life away from you.
Or, I have been leading the new life, but away from you.
If I could I would plagiarize from music, for instance.
Also I would send you pure tones or defend a form or try to live

Or trick and manage you as if you had been asleep.
It is a criticism of life or a criticism of death more exactly.
Whistler and Mallarmé's correspondence has not been translated
But when it is, you will note "my Mallarmé" as an expression.

One might call it tracing a hyacinth, or traces of a hyacinth.
Like traces on a blackboard.
Or tracing the window from a neoclassicism upon a blackboard.
These days that might as well not exist.

Amerikanische Lyrik, orange and red and yellow green.
Blind and sleeping and angry nonimitations, flowers.
I could not draw, so I sketched this soundless one of hopelessness.
Between lives occur lamps.

CONCEALED WORDS II

Where is the dragon David dreamt he drove
poor pet, other letters are already exposed
If you build another word, that word may be stolen
a little later are the earliest violets
with Pythagoras thinking of violets as heartshaped blades
certain rules might be observed: adding *s* does not
        constitute the new
this applies to certain games, played alone but fun with two
but the palm could be stolen with an *s* to make a psalm

The black color at the bottom of the river
has seeped through the bridge and stained your dress
if the bridge were your necklace and the sky your neck
Nightwalkers aflutter at every word
in the alleged rain of blood
You passed over my body like shallow water
depositing me in the distance

Suppose you take any sentence the sentence One
cannot please all the world and his wife
Concealed words include plea and sell and ease
and perhaps a few more for you to start working
In any event, you will find concealed words
your musical memory is good

Loving to hide
Moving backward more readily than forward
with the juices of your prey
at the base of your self–made pit

But something disappears
Ice is called ice and the air curves
the horses munch in the electric field
The eye must form images if they are to be seen
It was when candles were placed inside the car
Though the flame will be deflected
and what happens to the string after it is cut
by the effort of flame?
The blind spot enters
And light falls forever humorously

As if I lived within a few feet of your bedroom window
Centers of human population not being what they should
The "staff of life" hollow except at joints
The monotonous calls continued through the hottest days
Like regions of ice with their semigems

Mother and Father and welsh terrier
and the house go hand in hand
pressing the loose snowflakes tightly

Heard melodies being an edge situation of sorts
those unheard are sweeter
Therefore, bird,
tunnel into the soft sky
into the sea caves, into the crevices,
into the day and the double nest.

A SPANISH PAINTING

I dreamt of you and told you I had a very realistic dream.
You told me you didn't like me even to dream with material of you.
I told you it used nothing but your unintentional smile
And the international situation of the author.

You told me not to start the tension all over again, as with
A diamond inside the eyes; Spanish painting; real clothes for ghosts;
Or like the title of a store, Gems and Junk.
I tried to remember the phrase, The motorcycles of the air.

First I had a lucid dream and got exactly what I wanted
Like an article of the magazine that rides on a subway
Or a series of books behind a cartoon like a carpet
Placed upon the gallery floor to make the taker mad.

You told me not to start the tension over again, as in bed.
The carpet, the page, covered the floor, as blinds the window, a river.

FROM MALAY

Indelible lust (for you)
Two persons, two dim hints
Craving you monotonously
Oh gymnast sparrow

Two persons, two dim hints
Like sugar in a summer bicycle basket
Oh gymnast sparrow
Asleep on your twig

Like sugar in a summer bicycle basket
The newly dead are easy to find
Asleep on your twig
If only life and death were an eggshell like Princess Eggshell

The newly dead are easy to find
Craving you monotonously
If only life and death were an eggshell like Princess Eggshell
Indelible lust (for you)

MEMORY OF THE PRESENT

Opening the knots of your braid,
I look upon a seething Atlantic
Behold, a luminous typewriter sails
into the air above the desk.
The desk likes to return to the thick forest
The autumn as a kind of reward.
Like whirling eraser fluid,
I have been blown far enough.
Here and there, Basic Spanish, Botany,
and a Panorama (Critical) of Proust.

It's hard to get desire on paper.
The earth pulls your body down.
It is time to fall. Galileo Galilei.
All of us have a special province;
all of us have the slight year;
all of us when properly excited
emit ceaseless atoms, housed
in a cabinet at night; most of us
have a body and with equal arms.
Stone fruit is fleshy fruit: cherries.

You must be as it were an evening star
As Sappho says in her *Ode to Hesperus*
through which variegated ivies were women,
flakes of likeness, lines of ice.
December follows November, as I follow
My soul is seeping through your braids like water
from the mirage of the November pool.
Hic et nunc
You have been before and remember it now
Sinking away with the same tone
You hate the flow, and yet it flows.

A REALISTIC BAR AND GRILL

The play is one paragraph;
the performance is something else.
Would you be interested in seeing
            the play?
So we descended to meet
In the old opinions
Having given up nothing
Clothed in Joseph's serape
Stepping on a nonreferential ladder
Each rungless rung
The gentle cobra is dead
Everything that is me would rush
            up and meet you
Like the front of a subway
Rushing into a cave painting
The body is constantly going wrong
A mountain is social, but political
            I don't know
Like the library of "I don't know" books
He was always translating the *Oresteia*
            in three accents
Unjustly abused
As before unjustly celebrated
It wasn't the lionization
            of John Clare
Nothing naive and negative
Just air and pomp
Pomp and circumstance and
            circumstantial air

Shelley was a fire balloon
Or Shelley was a fire balloon lover
The first is launched among
                mountains
And the second drowns in
        a dull historic terrain.

AN EXAMPLE OF WORK

1

The bluejay is bobbing out in the yard, as if amusing itself
      with a country dance
That is a line you say that will produce guffaws in the Church
Well, first I saw a phrase in the dictionary *amusing herself*
      with a   the contredanse
And then I wanted to use the verb "bobbing"

And also I wanted to use the bluejay
And then I put in the backyard and I
      could see the bluejay
And so I — I forget. I what? Stole the bluejay?
You didn't hear me.

Your mind and tongue were sober, but your legs were intoxicated.
  That's about the bluejay.
Let us roll all our sweetness into a ball
like the hedgehog and go bristling
in every direction: the urchin.
Or rather, let us roll all our sweetness into a ball
      like the bluejay

I wrote all-out sweetness into a
Let us roll all-out sweetness into a ball.

By this point, one needs something calm and real
as the unabridged Oxford English Dictionary
      unabridged yet photoreduced
Unlike the bluejay but not unlike you
Who say nothing like, Let us roll all out sweetness up

However we are all rolled up, in an accident in a snowstorm
In my parents' home.   I look out the breakfast window
In the yard the bluejays are bobbing about, as if amusing
       themselves with a contredanse
Or country-dances, each sweet as an urchin.

2

Like an Eskimo in an umiak
   For the umpteenth time in the sunny ice
We go everywhere and sabotage
   With our silky blue sails and attacked by the air

   Let us roll all-out sweetness into a ball

As Taurus contains the Pleiades
   And the taste buds lie on the tongue
You enjoy this Indian Ocean
   Taking a small part in your mouth, three minutes to twelve

   Let us roll all our sweetness into a ball

You are playing Czerny in private
   And I the lowest man in the Marine Corps
You are nothing but morning
   Sound in air or fever in a disease

   Let us roll all-out sweetness into a ball

We are on either side of an open boat
   Carried in the waist of another ship
Temporarily supported by the delights of the rope
   Set in relation to the wind

   Let us roll all-out sweetness into a ball

That was when I wandered toward you
   Like a purple-faced wanderoo (and tufted macaque)
Three minutes to twelve
   Sunset on moon

   Let us roll all-out sweetness into a ball
   Let us roll all our sweetness into a ball

VALEDICTION CAPRICEN

The hope chest was filled with matches and
    cortisone and wallets
Gum and old voices, deferred dejections,
    probable hope,
Lightly bound copies of hopelessness, too,
    and circling hoots
From your lips beyond the diorama: weeds
    welded together.
One branch is a jungle, one white dress
Of the bright tree veracity as the sparrow
    fastened to a twig
How we apples swam, quietly,
    amicably
And now more than misrepresented, dirty
    time you covered with paint.

What Diomede is to the District of
    Columbia
Or the Dnieper to the submerged
    sandbank, so I to you tonight
Unsteady now from the triple effects
    of standing tiptoe in death
Like the highest point of a tirade,
    as air drains and birds alone
    are given knowledge
It was the future impressed on an
    handkerchief
The way Christ had a legendary
    cloth
Those were the harmless nights of
    phrases

You in your slip like a monk in quoins
        of stone: a blank leaf or inter-
        leaf

The unmerciful battering of your heart
        in my hand
Like the hands of fanatics destroying the
        classic beautiful faces
Because seen now as faithless being:
        portrait of the wind,
Your hair falls like an inventory on
        your breast
Fine, in what sense fine? Hmm?
Cut to death by mob action with legal
        sanction
Like the lyre of Orpheus and Mercury
        containing Vega
A sexually inviting throw of the dice
An animated cartoon of Paradise
A pastel jealousy of unusual
        depth
The lustre of one's confinement
The death of a young woman here rests
        on a couch

Holidays and congresses, planets and groups
        of stars,
Spain and the Citizen King
Creeds and confessions
Lamb of God who takest away the sins of
        the world — Capitalize all these.
I love you and the sun used as a saddle
        for women

51

In which the rider sits with her legs
    on the same side of the sun
And the sunrays split their sides
And pedestrians cannot tickle themselves
    for fear of fainting in the filaments
Of that heat   Oh slender worm
You are liable and I pay tribute
A leopard in a leotard in an Asia once I
    saw
It was an African one with buff black spots
    and on that leotard were scurfy
    scales

But you have been removed like a bugle
    in a drum
And I speak ineptly like a not so robust
    bee with hair
Cheerful, the middle part of a sail
Though a sail summoned to appear
    before court
Heaven becomes you
Ill as a token in a jet
Hat in hand you strolled the buildings
Big and forbidden and fern-like you
    fall
It's an odd sight I don't have of you
    tonight:
The red pen lies near the red Sphinx
The sky is covered like a tent for
    animal acts, the comb is silent
No word from the radiant white business
    paper as of yet
Nympholepsy, hateful word

That wave about to break in thick
        paint was the dud
But what about the wave before it
        the ghostly precursor
That was before you discovered jealousy
        in the dictionary

With a silver green dust of war in your
        hair
As twilight fills me up or is it
        midnight now sickened
Like an old story dunked into that
        silver green dust
Inextricably bound like Hofmannsthal
        and Richard Strauss
A silver brain in a silver ashtray
The rests are coming faster now
And sleep uncropped comes longing to be
        firmly fixed
And that is pine tar and fossils to you
The rising again to life of all my
        human dead
Shrouds from a ship's mast a clement ship
But the fruit has turned to rind
I cut you off and dress for burial

Unaccommodated man without an
        umbrella
Is an umbrella radiating from the
        weather itself
With a largely gelatinous
        structure if of storms

The umbrella forms the chief part
     of the body like the mind in a
     barrage
You cannot see what chords play
     on this disc
A branch of physical theory: diamond
     shaped in sorrow
The side of the horse's hoof which
     does not kill
The playing time of some games is
     divided the clement ship
Sweetest love, we are like the
     typewriter and the eraser fluid
Not the lexical meanings but
     like *altus,* high and low
Dolly Madison is an ice cream now
     and then: a garden
No suspects, no motives, no
     weapons
The water juts into the water
Not to know that pretty doesn't mean
     small that allegro means happy

The double negative like double-
     jointedness
Forming your name or a part of your
     name
Like a secret wine poured out in
     sleeping rooms
You lie like a coat of arms in my
     arms
Gurgling, to make a sound like that

The girlfriend of a gangster, small and
        slimy and elongate
Evergreens were creeping over New
        Jersey
La Capricieuse like the *Twenty-fourth
        Caprice*
Rarely if ever have there been such
        castles on stamps
Such harbors on a postcard
You harbor me emphasizing the a priori
        conditions
Taking the old paint off like moss on
        brick

The caprices slender as a woman's
        waist — you tremble
Holidays and congresses, planets
        and groups of stars
Your name or parts of your name —
        Capitalize these.
The water jutted into the water
        like a penis.
The tapered part of a wave
        painting
Converted into air, into fresh
        air —
Syllables inserted to fill a
        vacancy as *it* in *it was easy to
        say*
It does not keep the audience from
        seeing into things: the
        immaterial pyramid of
        those desires

You in your variable silk of
    deep purplish blue
Converted into air, into fresh air —
Floating toward the person who had
    fallen into it.

WHITE NIGHT

The earth is an isometric hexagon
and your will like a bolt head
and your forehead out of all size and now cut out
and the earthlight thrown upon the moonlight in full and half size

and the professional pictorial hexagons in the moonlight
and all this for an illustrator
and I no illustrator towering above you
as if you were cut out in increments, ellipses, acids

And the earth a small ellipse now
your accurate hands
and your black and white and red retina
and your breasts in gold and grease oil and salt

And your eyes in the major axes the pinpoint
of the desired diamond distance
your eyes sliding easily along the edge
tilted away from me in the dimensionlessness

How I searched for you through the precise pinholes
through the projections and the black holes with little events
which do emerge and the brain with its curves
and the large black circles that do not stop like an organic
      industry of the eye in this flow and this factory of a chart

You contained all the mathematical numbers
the small Greek alphabet of black ellipses
and some of the logical symbols
now like music in the green plant and depicting all music
      as power and light music carrying the load

The violin the contact the instrument the forehead
like a grid now and a switch in space
auctioned off like a template
cut out your brain cut out in the air in the office for the
      architect now in sheet metal

The swan was fiber tipped the swan and Zeus
the swan dried instantly as Zeus exploded heat-proof
and Nausicaa and Cleopatra in brilliant robes
and Donald Duck too in moist plastic eraser erased the
      available individuals with their broad logo

But most of all you hated the dithyramb
Uncle Scrooge sketching the sketch markers
and the nephews leaking and washing and hinged like a metal box
over the abyss a swimming pool and all the nephews assorted colors

Cringing in the pale cherry
cringing in the red red violet
in the pale walnut sky now colored dark oiled as redwood
in the cool grey in the warm grey the black and the extra black

Blue palms and now blueprints and the maze a sunbeam yellow
      which could not thread
brown as a blueberry in the sunset pink
grape as a red clay in the arctic blue
and the shaded pink as indigo over the blueprint in
      the sun's sky blue maze

I picked up the pencil and I picked up dust
and I picked you up like a surface clean whilst working
the powder-filled pocket and I prepared for the tracing
tracing and retracing you as work smudging and blemishing

Made of the stainless shadow
The soft eraser has worn itself away
You kneaded me into any shape and removed the marks
as your body hanging to be erased your skin shady as a pencil

Soft skin was for blending
and you shaded me like shading pastel
under the beach umbrella designed for the sky's blue box
Body as if strong again body running on the marked beach

Now the day is easily erased
and the night completely removed to the film's matte surface
Night rolls out in turquoise
Night with its curled grip universal night and push button day

Incomparable white night
eliminating us like the typing erasures now opaque white
Night flow freely over me with your brush and pen
covering all the colors — covering anything

NAME

Sybil, a bag of leaves is a painting
As if a portfolio were hidden in a pianola
And the clock must go clockwise and man perpendicular
To a bag of leaves

The waves inside the body continue
Cancelled out in the clouds however with one's preferences
So Aeneas pursued the earth, a lawn marked with paper
You destroyed the painting, Sybil, but maintained the price

Here were dainties and light crimes
The creaking of iron, the clanking of a piano
Two names, one fate, the reverence upper air has for paper
Bags full of rain and snow, books full of breezes — we who refused
    now read our painting

Walking a little in Paradise
Hidden on Fortune's wheel like a perpetrator
You struck the secret strings
Probably no more noiseless than many who decry our presence

MALLARMÉ TO ZOLA

All of me is Mallarmé to Zola.
My dear colleague,
I have some fear that induction is an error.
It is Thursday night, you are in your house like a season.
The house cannot be moved, but the present moves
It is always a double observation: I believe
that places are not prices but you have rented
absent from Paris
a dagger of hands
I have seen your bitter farce and I thank you
with the bit of my heart that I still have
laughing that single laugh that is permitted some simple times
     Tell me if I trouble you and believe me yours
let us speak of paper and lacunae of silk
I suffered a lot receiving your volume
I press toward you, one of your very close readers.

The ceiling like a piece of paper without a poem
And bigger than any dress
Full of themes I could be tempted to describe
But eyes closed on the dresses
Like your book closed fastidious as a cloud
Like your will in its banal adventures among silk
The title like you small and complete

There is no point of view
I am just a word found
Placed like an epigraph and prevented from becoming a group
The skin of Nana, which we have all caressed in a crowd
That is the work of an organization I could admire

One cannot applaud the night or regret or like pressed pants
Do you want to know what a journal is
what an entrée is what Thursday tomorrow is
Jewels, spectaculars, menus
I have seen the bitter farce and I thank you
With the little bit of my heart I still have
Nana passes by like a slaughterhouse without transition
And like a sombre end of a book
Is it forced as I believe on purpose still
To make the taker mad I am your faithful Mallarmé.

SNOW

Since I was born in the city of Newark
Moment by moment a very fine snow has been falling.
On very few days has it stopped snowing in my sleep.
The snow has widened till it joins the roofs; elevators sink
Into it; in sleep I build snow fortresses.
The sleep I have slept is also snow —
Snow poisonous as underpainting in Spain —
Snow in the surface as wide as an exile —
Snow in the airplanes that almost touch your face —
I advise you not to paint it.
At the end of the street I hear a snowy song;
Snow birds are lost in Chinese white snow;
In a single night parts of the car have turned to snow;
Another car moves forward for science.
Snow has fallen into the old bottle of eraser fluid.

FLESH

*By which we pass into one another
and ourselves into ourselves, in
order to have our own time.*
                    Merleau-Ponty

The robot's flesh
The robot is three inches tall
Yet it has weapons in its breast
Nothing moves us like nature's robot

Firefly among the rotten honeysuckles
bright enough to make the legible illegible
beyond the smooth Venetian blinds
Rain has rotted the English violin

We met and we met
together they left garbage on the moon
as to the new society of the rubber stamp
the language shines, especially on your flesh

It is why we were hungry for Job's tears
and human parting was new and beige and lavender
and we gripped the silver weapons
at the foot of the purple ancients and their bright red tears

It is too wrought like iron
on purpose laid to make the taker mad
hidden in the desk: a stainless ruler
the funerary explosions passing into you to kiss the door

As you used to say Mother Where would you
be without me In the gutter
And stay there
Laughing at the old acrostics and your
    sunny designs without pastel

Others prefer *Le bon usage*
One slice of a condominium the bite on your breast
a joke in relation to no consciousness
There is nothing in the desk but flesh

I dreamt that Thomas Hardy's poem
came tottering by
I dreamt the Thomas Hardy
was a wisp of smoke

I dreamt that yonder a mother and her son
go tottering by
And love's annals faded into earthly attuneable
hoarfrost overwrought night

I dreamt we were together again pregnant again egg white again
gagged agape aghast in the egg
in the brutal desk and the silver ruler stainless
ruled us and the blue point of the razor sharp pens

Demons are unusually pleased
meeting their victim in pearls
Drop this letter into the
thought for me: you had many corners

The land of mystical peaches turned
into disappointed pyramids
hungry for your tears, for your pearls, for your corners
hot and healthy, Winter troubled us
hungry for the visits of the sick birds, hungry for the whitecaps

Now I am here by forcelessness of my own will
Not here, not here, not here, but elsewhere
Bound to aid all rebellions
run away into the clarity of the lack of truth known to the
    mistranslators
The truth is known to the mistranslators, known to the feeble like
    garbage on the moon

Known on the river passing before me like cars
I have sailed on it to please you
and break in half for you and plead for you
I would have sailed on it to think of you

FRIDAY NIGHT QUARTET

I

ST. BARNABAS

My mother said,
All surgeons want to do is surge.
And as one took the staples from her skull
She said, Neurosurgeons are not nice.

Mostly blind and leaning against a wall
She told my father, Irv, you can be replaced
God forbid I should sit where I want to sit,
And what's wrong with this chair pray?

Sitting and crying, she said
This is not Chekhovian
Or Tolstoyan, David.
This is annoying.

Lying on the angiogram cot, strapped down and hot
    and bloody,
My mother said, The worst words in the English language
Are these David — Don't move.
And what do you think the best words are: Here's some water.

My mother said,
I'm not wavery because I have a wall
And I love it —
Walls are convenient because they don't move.

One day I walked with a tube of toothpaste in my hand
And Debbie said What are you doing with the tube of toothpaste
I don't know I forgot to put it down
I noticed a slight look of contempt on Debbie's face

Poor Debbie
It must be awful to have a mother who's not very bright
Who asks you what day it is
As Michael and Noah would say Ech and Yuch

The other day we were expecting a new Maytag
And Willimae who's very bossy said
Oh Mrs. Shapiro the Maytag men are here
Put your wig on! For what? Ridiculous!

Sometimes Dad grabs my face and points me
In the direction he wants to go
And I say Why do I have to go in that direction
I usually respond, Well, go; he doesn't need me to help him
He's adamant about the direction he wants to go

The worst thing about a cardiovascular accident
Is not being able to walk up steps
I can walk around a room
But I can't walk upstairs

There are things in closets I've put away months ago
And I can't get up there to see them
Just clothes
And I can't get downstairs to the cellar to do the
        wash — a pillowcase full of dirty clothes

And Irv says Oh they're not dirty
But I think they are
And sometimes I ask Irv to put real hot water in the sink
        so I can take a sink bath
And he'll say You just washed

Don't get a cerebral vascular accident
If you can help it
Well maybe a long time ago I would have thought you could eat
     a lot of sweets and die of a high insulin reaction
But I wouldn't advise anyone to do that

Years ago I used to say I'm so lucky
If I want to get out of this thing all I have to do
     is eat one or two sundaes
And I'd have a diabetic coma
No problem

We sit and we listen to a lot of opera
Pavarotti sometimes Bjoerling Martinelli
The best thing I've heard recently is the Mozart quintet
with Heifetz and Piatigorsky and somebody Domingo

And I find myself crying because I never hear
     live music anymore
It's all canned
If you played here
It would be very much alive

Everybody loved my Dad because he laughed at everybody.
He had a magnificent laugh with tears
When comics came to South Africa they'd invite him
To sit in the front row — he'd laugh loudly

It was quite apparent to me that Pop was not laughing AT me.
And I would stand by the open window when I was 5
or 6 and pretend to be *davening*.
And he would laugh and laugh, this litle girl who was praying.

My mother said, If you have a beautiful speaking voice
You can count on a beautiful singing voice.
I used to imitate the little boys in his choir. I would give myself
a boy's nasal voice, and he would laugh.

Sleeping in Gideon's twin bed, and John's twin bed,
and Pop was telling me stories in Yiddish
About little tiny people who sleep in rosebuds.
All Pop's stories were about miniatures,
        mice who ate the crumbs or babies who sleep in rosebuds.
Little people
Nice families who had children so tiny they could hardly see them
and how happy they were with these almost unseeable
        people
He loved furniture that was too small for anyone to sit in
And then he would end with his famous two lines
They were famous because I didn't know what they meant,
A shetkl arain a shtekl arois
Di maise iz ois
Stick in, stick out
The story is finished.
It meant I couldn't nag him to tell me more, I was to go to sleep.
In. Out.
He never told me a story without ending it that way, ever.

II

THOSE WHO MUST STAY INDOORS

DESERT MISTLETOE

Wounds in rainy seasons may become badly infected
But you have many days left
Bones, flowers, March days, white days, days
Growing in the window, where you are grown a wandering Jew

Interesting animals seem to leap from nowhere
Give a confusing series of clacking croaks: A good test for hearing
    some do not hear it at all
Mr Frog lives within jumping distance of a permanent pool
All boys and girls should have a chance to learn about sleek snakes

Where ravens work cooperatively in the night
The stars and the maps and the horizons should now be rent
We mean a number of things, but chiefly we refer
To variations in brilliance, groups of stars, lines in the
    maps now dots

As soap and pie and bread are names for happy or unhappy
    combinations
So are the rocks
So-called seas are darker regions
Hands pulling the root out, twisting it easily from the moist ground
                             the night sky

"Upside-down bird and twirl-around-a-twig describe antics
Apparently liked by those who do not know your name
A visitor and beloved
By those who must stay indoors"

III

ORANGE-COLORED SKY

My mother said,
I couldn't keep my hand off your face,
I was always caressing your chin.
We used to listen to a television program, you and I,

And the guy sang a song called "Orange-colored Sky"
And his name was George. He'd say GEORGE.
So we wrote a letter to him, and I wrote it for you and I said
I am five years old and a classical musician
    who plays the violin

And I really prefer Bach and Beethoven
But I like the way you sing "Orange-colored Sky"
And he read it out loud to all the people in the audience
And you heard it, and he said, "This is a letter from
    a little boy, David Shapiro, Hopson
    Street, Newark," which got a laugh.

IV

FRIDAY NIGHT QUARTET

When we dead awaken we'll play chamber music Fridays
Even if wrecked sustain freezing death, still satisfied
She made me quiet, she will again
At a spell of longing, beyond boundaries of town —
    dying — urge — spike — bargain-ardor

Silent man takes a repeated test, a second photograph.
Rotten willow you have an abortive stem.
When one studies crime or the prevention of crime,
    the peony has no money
Dear flower, destitute and household god, my enormous
    youth beneath.

The air thirsts for water
And will accept from any object including your human skin.
Your brain upon bursting releases a shower of brilliant
    cartoon stars
Slowly but thoroughly you sucked the honeysuckle.

A war was in progress between the wasp and me!
Stinging me on the knee, it could only laugh and leave.
I know I shouldn't have thrown a music-stand at you
Moved merrily among midgets, slept a lot in humorous trees.

I sat in my room with these borrowed games
Blandly I steered my flanks toward the sea again
That foolish herbarium. But when I tried to pass
    into that vague life
The fish rose up in a transparent bloc against me.

V

FOUNTAIN

Too dizzy, too wavery to weep
puffy, bald, obtunded
blind mostly,
the so-called silent portion of the brain removed —
a believer in walls — "they cannot move" —
my mother was dying in her sleep
like a cloud that has slipped out of place
and rolled down the canvas sky
Dizzy, wavery, asleep,
how could she die?
That night I saw a fountain
inscribed with this advice
"Laugh loudly, love, as my voice laughs in the grey water."

VI

SESTINA

I asked my Mother for a new form
from Paradise. But all I could
see was a slight surface like the
old toy bowling balls that yielded
little answers. Struggling to see
something, I saw a sestina in lines of
color, like magic marker on a lake:

_____

_____

_____

_____

_____

_____

NOVEMBER TWENTY SEVENTH

My old desire to live

I've built nothing; you are the architect.
You are near me like the sound of an archaic car.
I know that I love the verb not to know.
Do you love it? The distance is like a Chinese garden.
I pluck pomegranates out of the Halloween stores.
Then I keep looking at this phrase like summer hills.
The mountain represents nothing, the mountain air
Represents nothing, but two birds seem bad enough.
In these things there is an immense exile like a surface:
And when we try to stop expressing it, words are successful.

I PACKED MY TRUNK FOR ALBANY

There is no kid in kid gloves,
There is no rice in rice paper.
You chose the words and wrote the final letters
And the missing letters were *letters* written in.

Column one spelled the moth eyebrows
Column four spells the coffee berry.
The coffee is not a berry
It was a seed spelled separately
     with its young.

Graze away, little ox,
While I spin your head and begin to doze in the
     dark Cossack wound.
It stood till the sun fell to pieces.
Take some, said the ox and the ox and the ox still tugged.

Who was the sleeper? Who lived in the shoe?
My bed is like a slightly disenchanted houseboat
I spy with my little eye a sense of touch.
I went to school and first thing I saw was a missing word.

Beginning with the missing
I was going to stop but I heard the missing word.
So I ran to my locker in the dark and I hung up my missing word.
I went to my room and spoke to the missing word.

SONNET

Ice over time

Loving your traces and loving to trace
teaching us tricks in the dusky light of your devices

On the margin of an indifference

Hippolytus Oenone travellers more or less
Absent of purpose on wings of chance
Neverness, sweetness, extraneous as the wind blows

The Alive with Pleasure sign has been torn down

replaced by Golden Lights in river haze
    a mild Lucretian signboard

perfumes novelties displays
    toying with you as you say Don't toy with me
      my favorite mouth my favorite grey pen
        I will pilot its razor point toward the page

TO A YOUNG EXILE

Surely it is more than inserting the word *word*
Over others descending in hell
Or rising in scum and mist to ask how one might love
    this physical disease
To that one whose sex is unknown and immaterial

Ice in the river and ice in the sky,
Ice in the negative and ice on the lens and the eyes
Ice and flowing past us, every part of our inorganic life,
    oxymoronically spent
Two nations after all like two birds frozen over in pastel dust over
    their little prey

They were not thinking we could see anything
But we did see the sentences running over and the
Two souls you had alas always housed in your breast
The house loves to be cut up

Exterior and interior exiles
I do see and I see also beyond this field of books
Fangs glittering
The nations destroyed simultaneously like fireflies

WRITING IN BED

Writing in bed
The houses at diagonals
Put on their solar collectors
But I don't want to collect
As if I finally wrote that song
"I just don't want to see the light"
Writing in bed
Watching your handwriting
To what did the Japanese poet
Compare the world?
To writing on this small day
No I have not yet died
Criticizing us in a sense
For needing a wave or a corpuscle
Writing in bed
Come into the Calderón life-is-a-dream
I loved you without an image
Without a future, without a reference
What do you represent, what
Are you a copy of
And now let someone else
Love you that way (after Pushkin)
Writing in bed
In a world where anyone can enter
Anyone's room by will
Escalators are easy
Self-reflexive as a bell
In the midst of sleep talk
But even limitlessness could not include
The limit, which is a confusion
Even a critique of gala white
Window white, empire
White, Horizon white

Writing in bed
As if you were medicine
Real as a placebo
Placed under the tongue to make
The taker mad —
Nevertheless, we move
Writing in bed
With a new favorite pen
I guess the soul changes
Its handwriting sometimes

"WHAT DOES BANKRUPTCY MEAN TO YOU"

A piano, a violin and a piano
a violin lies rotting on the piano
in a new night which is not there
The piano speaks only of architecture
the violin speaks only of poetry

You did say you understood it must be painful
I loved the whirlpool
I loved the "crude and brutal forms"
Of mist, ice and mist suspended at a considerable height
Not wishing to be known as a transported criminal in America

I do not even exist, and I like it
In love with a tunnel
The more you are in a tunnel, the less you are
Withdraw half the funds
Deeply in love with a tunnel

TO PAINTING

A host of golden pencils
and *MIND* a quarterly review
I see you like roses on television
crouching with thoughts about this obscure life

Lagging behind like frost on the window
while others are at the core of a vista
as if police could be summoned for this sad soul
with the worn-out look of a grafted rose

On the window sill the window birds
fan their wings to the air-conditioner
after a specious summer interval
and Heifetz plays *Le Plus que Lent*

We were the higher ones
and the travesty you can never forget
To be followed by shining blackberries
It was certainly a peaceful walk with only the occasional shepherd

Now the worst of not being a botanist
Was this, for instance, the end of my poor plant?
Like a pot in which the rose is received
By enemies of the rose.

Revenge made
no sweeter by the site of its celestial résumé
The *Scherzo Tarantelle* is finished
The reference to Enrico Fermi on a little boat is hard to forget.

TO THE DEAD

Pots and pans of classical Athens
how the pots looked in antiquity
and how the ancients regarded the abundant pans, etc.
The pots have not changed appreciably
but the pans, though mild, were ever rigorous
The pot that shivers in the March wind
or the pans that scorch in August heat
are only enduring the excesses that made Athenians tough soldiers
and courageous crockery
Thus Homer alludes to the black pan on the sea
and the silver trickle of water over a cliff into a pot
Their awareness of landscape is apparent in their sites
for pots and pans, their love of knives
In the pot flourish all trees
pears and pomegranates, and apples full of fault
Beyond the last rows of pots and pans
well-laid detective plots have been arranged
blooming all year with black flowers, black pots and pans
To gush out beside the stately palace
from it we citizens draw our water, and our rocky escapes
To you, Priapos, this curved sickle thirsts
And Plato taught in the garden, where the pot whispered
   love to the pan
and the throats of the naturalists were cut down
This must have been in a wet spot near the Great Drain
a tiny fountain devastated the garden, the microcarpus, its regal
   spears
Mauve white ghosts marching on the fields of asphodel
Probability, the most carefully tended garden

I CANNOT HOLD NOR LET YOU GO

I am no longer afraid of the darts
Nor are they of me darting into the tenebrosa
I am surrounded by a quirk by a peroration of a question
very much in evidence among the olive trees and the darts

Now you know why I let you emend me so
like a template on a horizon
when the mind inclines to an abhorrence
and the mitre inclines on the desk of the architect

She is stepping lightly as fuzz over the hay of the world
and hawkweed what is more or less dying out over orange laughter
and the ceiling is speechless with a respect

and the mitigated circumstance asks now of today
what are you doing tomorrow on the hacienda
Could it be you know I'm still living, leashed to the hateful sky.

TO THE PAGE

The page is not a deep wood
nor is it a wooded ravine
nor is it a log though it is a slight cavity
lined with moss and sometimes the leaves of your hair

The page, the page! The black page too is valuable
The little page swallowed me up
whole and crushed me afterwards
The hours like smoke trees

The page in the Connecticut River
The page in nothern New York
like the moist decaying woods
the page haunted by hillsides and violins and ravines

Oh page I walk about the ground
searching for food and the like
but you have no special interests
scattered rather than concentrated,
     with a secret like that of the sparrow

THIN SNOW

Screens in a dream,
grey blinds,
robots toying with a tree's model,
images of images,
worlds, not quite, taking a bath of time today,
your face on the music stand,
sedentary mentalisms,
quotations, dissertation on,
family carving,
travesties —
are torn paper,
doubt like looping wire,
a buried city for color,
the river tears space
the inside of broken chalk,
nothing is behind poetry
though it hollows the page
And so the snow fell
and covered up poetry.

FOUR LINES

Forced to sing O History
What you need is mimesis
A boy and Psyche once
Came together in a dream

A boy and Psyche once
Came together in a dream
Forced to sing O Mimesis
What you need is history

In a dream David and Psyche
Came together
Forced to sing O History on a bridge
What you need is a bridge

Cupid and Psyche once
Came together in a well
What you need is limitation
"Oh mastery"

I don't mind height if I see
Such ships bridge sky and water
A boy and Psyche once
What you need is imitation O forced to sing

THE OTHER AND THE OTHERS

I wanted to paint the night sky
Too easy to make a black xerox

You are Persephone with a torch
In you the slenderness of the end of the century

I would have my own boat
Sailing homewards, it would never turn back,
        under the wide lack of sky

Oh slighly incline your worn body towards
            me
Above you the hollow airplane quivers

Full of life like a lie
The medium again correction fluid

Stamped into many light stars
Too many would be impossible: the wound so
        wide

To visit you now
In paradise, full of the acutely ill

A double flute of life scraped away
A knife pushes through the earth

You no longer
Protect me, as wire protects a tree

To enter Liberty's body, a copy of a copy!
As a noiseless plane, a worm, dove into its
        casket

SCHEHERAZADE SCHOOL SCREEN

It was Act Four
of Junior Fun in Bed
Discovered like an incinerator room
in the incinerator room and passing through
        lines and circles to New York.

You could only pass through each vapid circle once,
and the horrible journey ended
no matter what route you took in New York.
It was hot for January, warm for the dumbly thankful dog
        beside the kitchen range.

The American bird ate up
the evening meal.
The crossword puzzle was a bird cage and the bird exclaimed
with disgust and pain the first person singular of "to be."

The human body
was a black hole.
Of course, that was the real trouble between the colonies
and the Mother country.

Two important acts were found concealed here
but when you found them out
you forgot them: taxation without representation, and
        representation without you, without the rubbed-out
        couch, the nickname, the plural pronouns.

Take this silk and make me a linoleum rug
And on this linoleum let there be a book embroidered
Such a book as the world has never: Home soaked through with rain
And none the better for it, and the letters set to work, and
        in less than an hour they had the linoleum ready.

Thirty years has September
No I don't that's it like a vase trembling
in the lucent mistranslation of
page ninety-nine: realm without a cause.

It was hot for January.
And its neighbors lay drifting past the
butterflies upon the dead glaciers
with the smugglers and the answers to the puzzles that were to
     break the monotony.

And the answers came drifting in
as if the human body were a black hole
And two acts that lay concealed had caused it all:
the trouble beween the colonies and the Mother country.

Taxation without representation
is tyranny and representation
is tyranny.

Quo Vadis presents
planning agendas and rainbow systems
and rainbow planning systems

black pocket systems also for planning
and shopping macadam madams
and little notes rejected after all

Paper will be distributed
and your desk will be the indispensable
Think of paper
and you will be taken

to the oblique at your feet
grating and
waiting for crayons and pencils and style
The telephone has its repertoire and Poulenc plays Poulenc
     Narcissus erases the flower with a whirling hand

Memory helped you
like an extra plate
and the years helped you
like a luxury gained from leather

and the amnesia helped you
one week to a page
And the hypermnesia helped you
two days to a page, one month, one day, one fact,
     a single value organizing the whole summer shore

It was time that satisfied the Queensbury rules
Time that oscillated to the music like quartz
Time that inquired about the quibbles and the quarantines
And time that hid the present like a birthday present

My eyes were cut
I saw each leaf as if with new glasses
The streep lamps rose like grandmothers beside the beach
I was called to be that one without a vision in the time
     that smirked and smeared so much purple on nature

The future the scum of the earth as sculpture seagreen and
full of doubts
I followed you but you escaped into the screen
as if to pamphleteer or inquire

THE NIGHT SKY AND TO WALTER BENJAMIN

Best to use a dead and nervous language
The extraordinary effort will do nothing
The sun is so close to us
The moon of Pluto even the newspaper's moon of Pluto
so far away
The one thing Hamlet did not mention
is that things might get better
In the clear sea a little glass pulverized for my pleasure
You do your griefwork, dreamwork, like homework
Someone lost his money in the night sky
Someone cut into the shape of dice
threw the dice against unbounded odds
light from falling dice

NAME AND ADDRESSES

Pythagoras said,
Upon rising from bed

Obliterate the print of your body
Innocent archaeology!

Rats surround us
And we call them squirrels

If they had thinner tails
We'd call them rats

Guilt is longer than love
Longer and stronger than love

Philodendron
And the rats live on

Vibrant disclosure
and deadly closure. Of the door.

Even sleepers
Are workers

And collaborators
Electrons that once loved each other

TO THE EARTH

for Meyer Schapiro

I fell with my father through space
In a space module as round
    as your thumb

My father remarked of the earth
How they had divided everything

By twos or by one (a joke)
It was better by far to visit the other side
    than stay stranded in that self

We passed the poor Americas
    South Africa striped as a zebra
And Russian artists who could not practice their art

The art of the grid
While others wondered whether we had seriously
    judged the grid

But all over the earth the artists painted
    what they wanted
Except where they could not — or what they needed —
    and did not

And my father worried aloud
Knocking on the moonlit plastic module door

When we fell, we screamed
But we were safe in Texas, safe as Texas, safe
    as Texas in Texas

Eating bread not electrons
Madly in love with the earth.